PIANO · VOCAL · GUITAR

CHRIS_TOMLIN
BURNING_LIGHTS

ISBN 978-1-4803-1872-4

HAL•LEONARD® CORPORATION
7777 W. BLUEMOUND RD. P.O. BOX 13819 MILWAUKEE, WI 53213

Visit Hal Leonard Online at
www.halleonard.com

Burning Lights

Words and Music by CHRIS TOMLIN,
DANIEL CARSON, JESSE REEVES
and JASON INGRAM

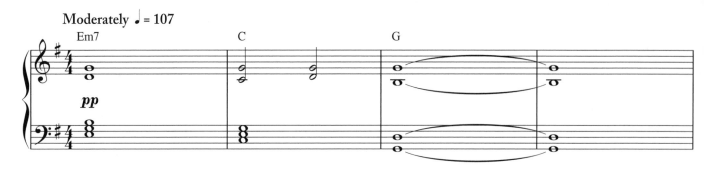

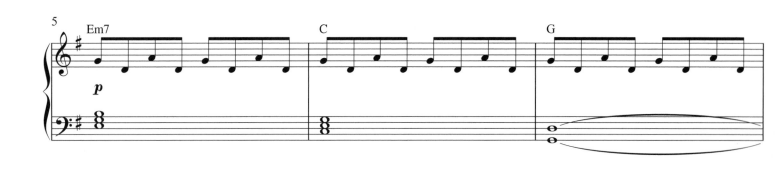

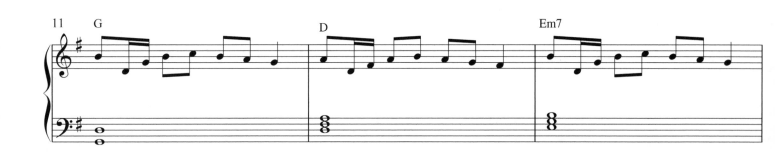

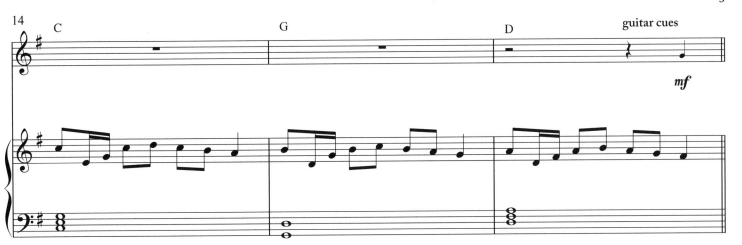

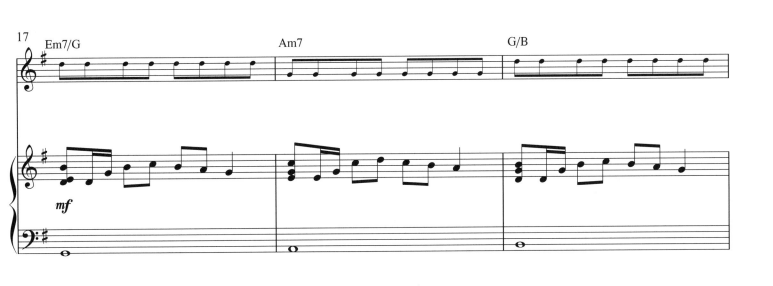

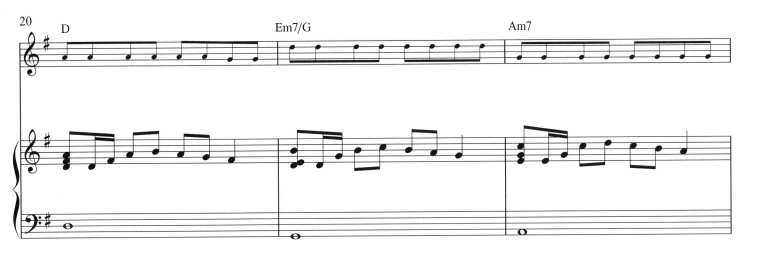

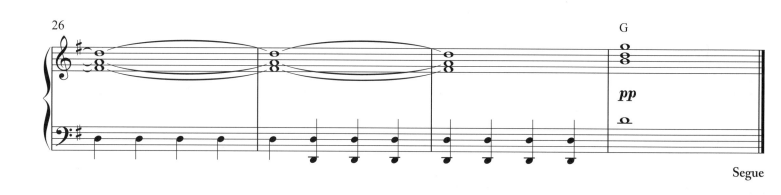

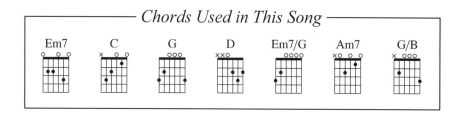

Segue

Chords Used in This Song

Awake My Soul

Words and Music by CHRIS TOMLIN,
DANIEL CARSON, JESSE REEVES
and JASON INGRAM

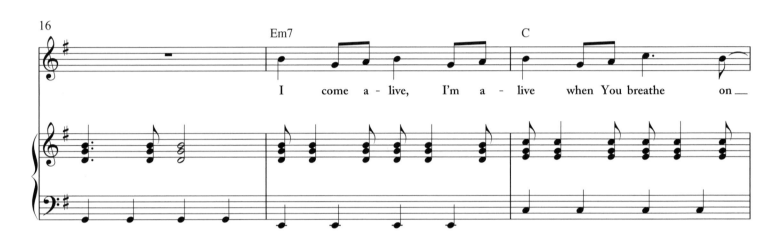

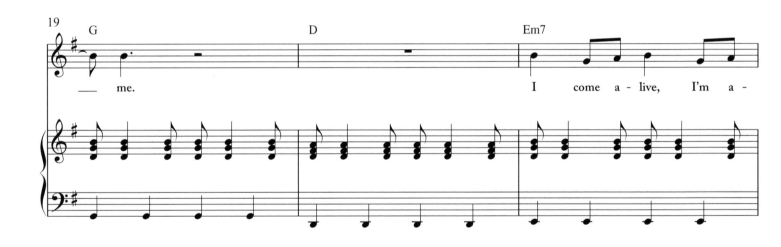

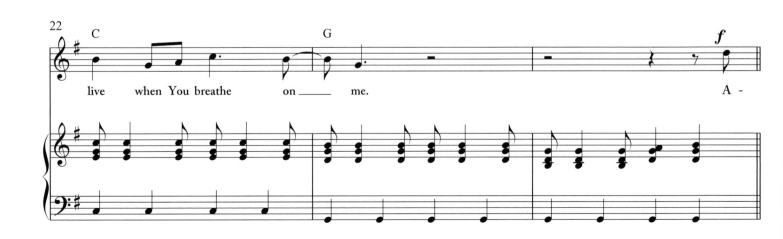

Spoken Lyrics

And then He said to me, "Prophesy to these bones and say to them: Dry bones, hear the word of the Lord.
This is what the Sovereign Lord says to these bones. I will make breath into you, and you will come to life."

So I prophesied as I was commanded. As I was prophesying, there was a noise—a rattling sound.
And the bones came together, bone to bone. And I looked, and the tendons and the flesh appeared on them,
and skin covered them. But there was no breath in them.

And then He said to me, "Prophesy to the breath. Prophesy, son of man, and say to it:
This is what the Sovereign Lord says. Come from the four winds, O breath, and breathe!"

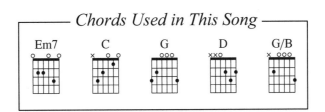

Whom Shall I Fear
(God of Angel Armies)

Words and Music by CHRIS TOMLIN,
ED CASH and SCOTT CASH

VERSE 1

1. You hear me when I call. You are my morn-ing song.

Though dark-ness fills the night, it can-not hide the light. _____

CHORUS

I know Who goes be - fore me, ___ I know Who stands be - hind.

The God of an - gel ar - mies is al - ways by my side.

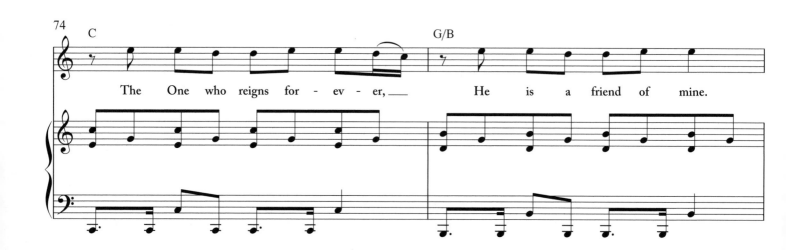

The One who reigns for - ev - er, ___ He is a friend of mine.

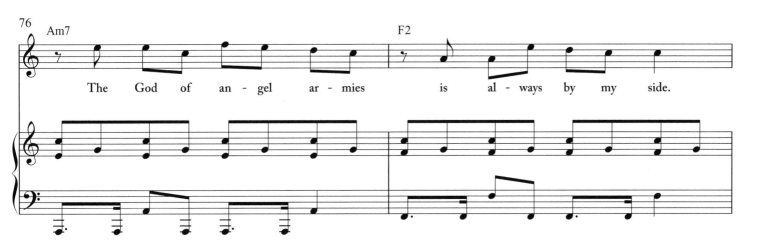

The God of an - gel ar - mies is al - ways by my side.

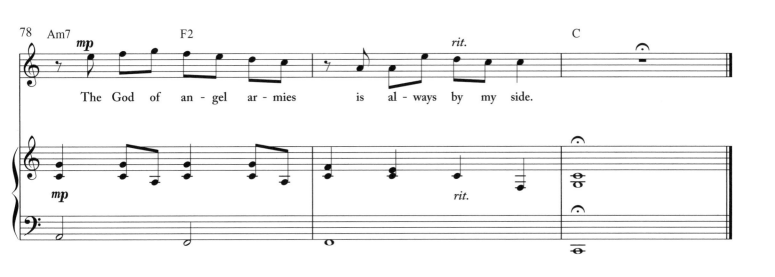

The God of an - gel ar - mies is al - ways by my side.

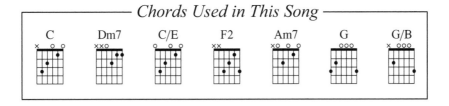

Chords Used in This Song

C   Dm7   C/E   F2   Am7   G   G/B

Lay Me Down

Words and Music by CHRIS TOMLIN,
MATT REDMAN, JONAS MYRIN
and JASON INGRAM

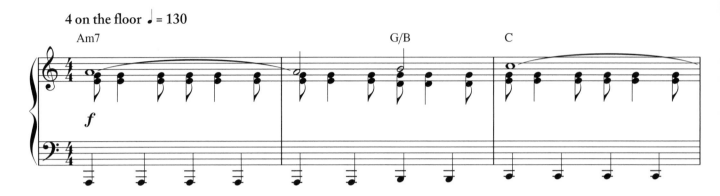

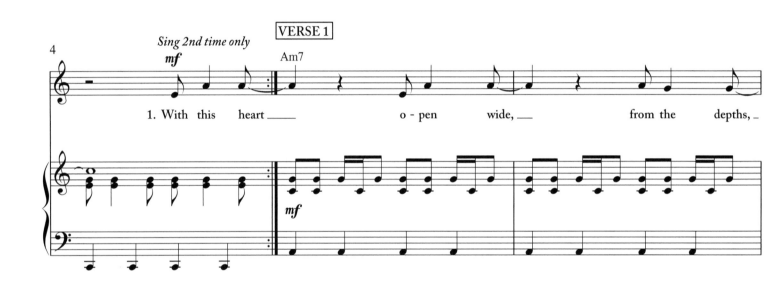

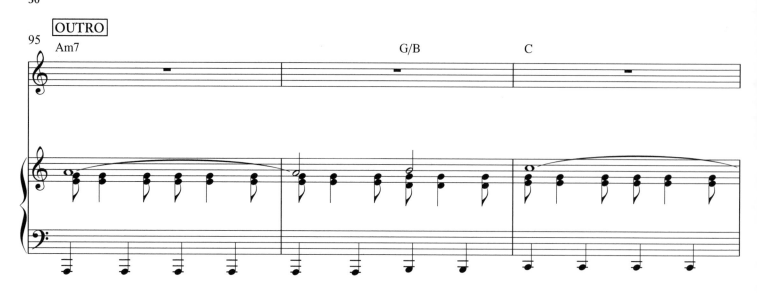

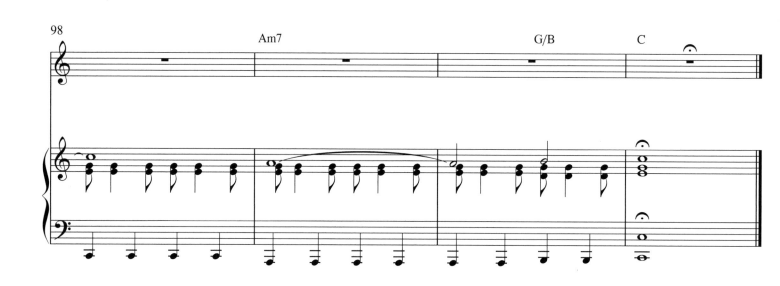

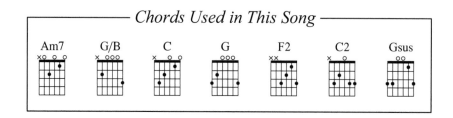

God's Great Dance Floor

Words and Music by CHRIS TOMLIN,
MARTIN SMITH and NICK HERBERT

I am a-live on God's great dance floor!

OUTRO

Chords Used in This Song

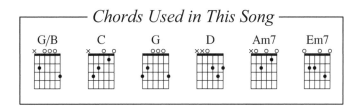

White Flag

Words and Music by CHRIS TOMLIN,
MATT REDMAN, MATT MAHER
and JASON INGRAM

CHORUS

BRIDGE

Chords Used in This Song

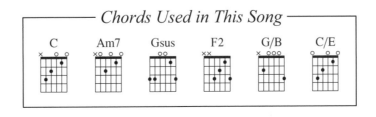

Crown Him
(Majesty)

Words and Music by CHRIS TOMLIN,
MATT MAHER and ED CASH

Capo 1 (C)

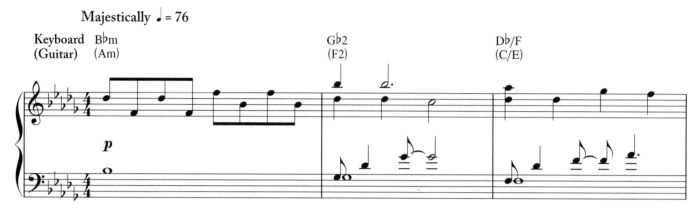

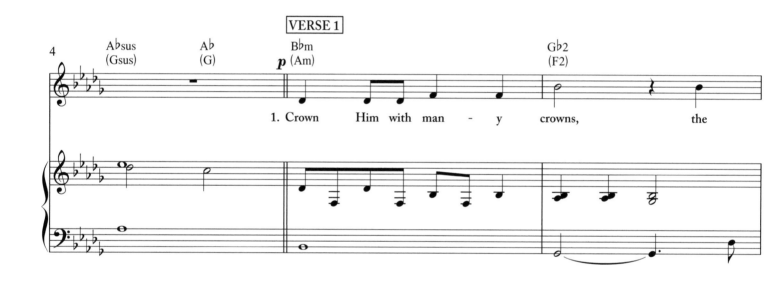

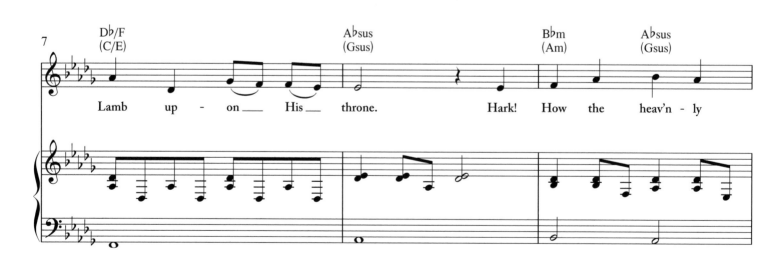

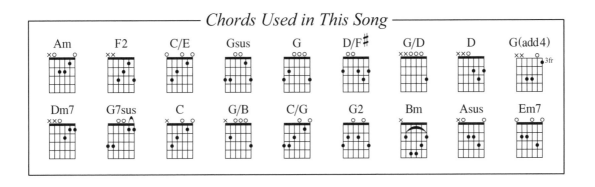

Jesus, Son of God

Words and Music by CHRIS TOMLIN,
MATT MAHER and JASON INGRAM

Sovereign

Words and Music by CHRIS TOMLIN,
MARTIN CHALK, MATT REDMAN,
JONAS MYRIN and JASON INGRAM

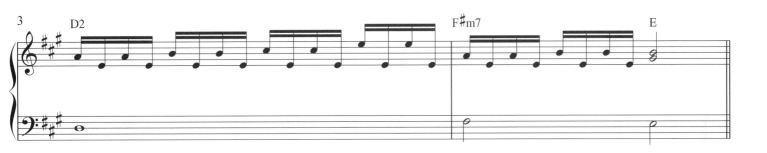

L.H. 8vb 2nd time

L.H. as written both times

OUTRO

God, what - ev - er comes my way, I will trust You.

Chords Used in This Song

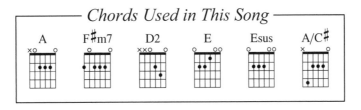

A   F#m7   D2   E   Esus   A/C#

Countless Wonders

Words and Music by CHRIS TOMLIN,
ED CASH and MATT ARMSTRONG

Capo 1 (G)

With wonder ♩ = 82

VERSE 1

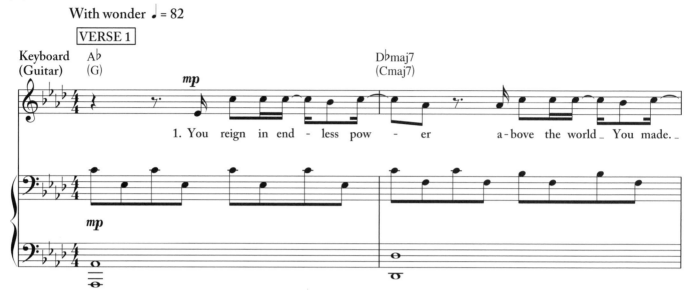

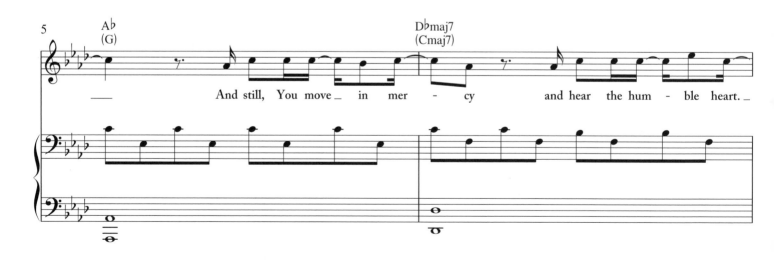

Great God of count- less won- ders, I will lift my __ eyes. __

OUTRO

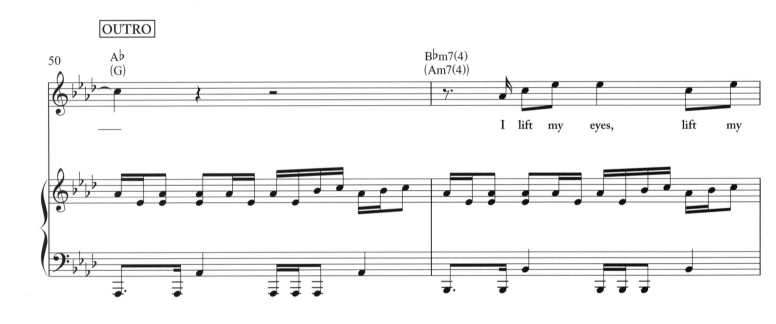

__ I lift my eyes, lift my

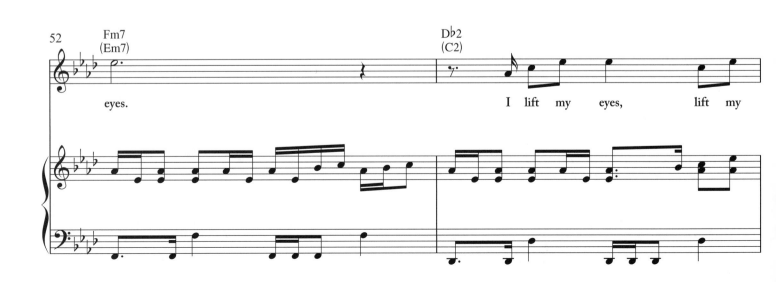

eyes. I lift my eyes, lift my

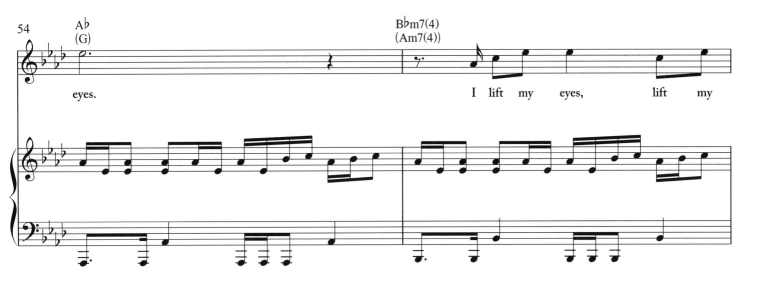

54

Ab
(G)

eyes.

Bbm7(4)
(Am7(4))

I lift my eyes, lift my

56

Fm7
(Em7)

eyes.

Db2
(C2)

Ab
(G)

Chords Used in This Song

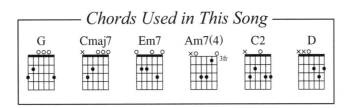

G   Cmaj7   Em7   Am7(4)   C2   D

Thank You God for Saving Me

Words and Music by CHRIS TOMLIN
and PHIL WICKHAM

CHORUS

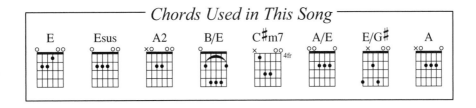

Shepherd Boy

Words and Music by CHRIS TOMLIN
and MARTIN SMITH

OUTRO

51 ff

Love   is a fi-re.   Love

54

is a fi-re.   Love   is a fi-re.____

57

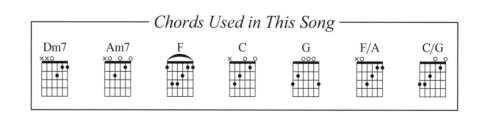

Chords Used in This Song

Dm7   Am7   F   C   G   F/A   C/G